31 Days

Of

Transformation

and

Character

Development

By
Curtis Whiteman

31 Days of Transformation and Character Development
Copyright © 2022 by Curtis Whiteman
All rights reserved.
ISBN: 978-1-0880-2865-0 (softcover)
ISBN 978-1-0880-6339-2 (eBook)

Unless otherwise indicated, all Scriptures quotations are taken from the King James Version of the Holy Bible.

Requests for information can be sent to: ProphetWhiteman@Gmail.com

Printed in the United States of America

Endorsements

It is a great honor and an esteemed privilege to offer my endorsement for this insightful devotional written by my friend and brother Curtis Whiteman. Not always do you find individuals that have the commitment and dedication to aid others on their spiritual journey. However, the insight and honesty offered by this writer can lead anyone searching for God into a consistent and dedicated walk with Him. This devotional is clear and direct with a focus on not just learning the Father and His will for our lives, but to propel anyone to consider or reconsider ourselves. To do a serious self-reflection and know who we are, whose we are and what is our purpose in Him. We all need to gaze in that mirror from time to time and check to see if we are on the right track and going in the right direction. I believe that anyone who picks this devotional for their growth in God and takes it seriously will be emersed and enlightened into a well of encouragement, comprehension, and hope. I commend Prophet

Curtis for having the courage to share his heart with others for their evolution and continued success in God. My best to his every endeavor and my prayers for his latest work.

Humbly Submitted,

Rev. Joseph J. Jones, Senior Pastor of the Mount Hermon BC
Bachelor of Theology, Lighthouse Christian College
Master of Divinity, Lighthouse Christian College
Master of Theology, Lighthouse Christian College
Master of Divinity, Lighthouse Christian College

How often have we been told to do exactly that but without any proper instruction as to WHY or HOW to accomplish this lofty yet vital mandate? The WORD of GOD tells us that men ought to always pray and not to faint but Rev, Curtis Whiteman walks into the WHY and HOW of prayer by taking us by the hand to unfold the art and science of prayer. True prayer is birthed from devotion; hence it is the exact reason this book is a PRAYER DEVOTIONAL. Reverend Curtis Whiteman takes on a daily step-by-step expedition into the treasure chest of prayer, each devotional gives a prayer focus, a prayer guide, and a tour into the supernatural realm. Read this book with an open heart and you will come out with a hunger and a thirst to talk to GOD with honor and complete honesty. Expect not only a revival in your prayer life, but a revolution because of developing the heart, language, and necessity of praying to GOD every day, Rev. Curtis Whiteman's passion for prayer is going to ignite an inextinguishable fire and passion for intimacy with your Heavenly Father.

Dr. Lenore A. Artis, CEO
L.A. Artis Ministries IAAWP, New York, NY
Master of Theology, Lighthouse Christian College
Bachelor of Theology, Lighthouse Christian College

As I read a snippet of Prophet Curtis Whiteman's Daily Devotional I was really inspired - not that I do not already follow the principles that he has shared, but to know that for someone who does not know God, or for the believer who is struggling with issues in life, this devotional would help either person grow closer to God and their God-given purpose in spite of what is going on in their life. The Bible is our road map to our journey in life and just like how we would use a GPS to navigate us around to where we need to go this daily devotional will help navigate the readers through their spiritual journey in life. I give my congratulations to Prophet Curtis Whiteman for taking the time out and authoring this book that will help so many far and near. I Pray it makes Best Seller on every platform that it is placed on because of the purpose that it was written.

Prophetess Nicole Bryant
Brooklyn, NY
Greater Temple of Praise
P.U.S.H Pushing Until Shifting Her LLC Founder and CEO
It's Your Time! Pushing forward with Nicole Radio show

Prophet Whiteman is providing in his book a step-by-step guide for the believer to take their spiritual discipline to the next level. He brings scriptural and practical spiritual exercises to help believers see that practice makes permanent. I recommend this book for anyone who wants to strengthen their faith and learn how to implement their faith in their everyday life.

Pastor Davon Felton
Emerge City, Jacksonville, Florida

Preface

The Lord led me to author this book. On my personal phone, I collected scriptures in my notes that I used as lessons for my daily living. I believe in living by the principles of the Word of God, because without obedience to God's word we would be lost, and in danger. I believe that every Christian believer should be biblically sound. When I say that, I am saying that as a follower of Christ we should know the principles of our faith. Those principles are discovered in our bibles.

This book is a collection of a few of my favorite scriptures, and they are accompanied by daily activities to exercise the principles discussed in the scripture. The word of God, if applied is a life-changing book for all those willing to be changed. I want you to embrace the scriptures, lessons, and practices enclosed in this manuscript. Our God has a great future in mind for each of us; let us make sure we are developed completely and prepared for what God has planned for us.

Dedications

Bishop Saint Christopher Zebedee Dowtin III

You were my friend, brother, and mentor. I prayed over me and prophesied to me. Many of the things I have begun to do you have spoken it into existence. I would tell you, "You are crazy, I cannot do that, and that will never happen." But many of the things you spoke to me are coming to pass just as you said they would. I am thankful God connected us when he did because the truth is if God did not do it when he did, I am not sure where my life would be. You left during a major shift in my life and many days I still cannot believe it.

My friend I miss you and I love you. (SIP)

Raymond Kelly Sr and Denise Kelly

I have watched the two of you support and love each other publicly and privately. As I pursued marriage, your example set the bar for my marriage. Your marital union has been an excellent example of supporting one another through personal and professional ups and downs. My prayer is that God will continue to bless your marriage and grant you the desires of your heart.

Pastor Jeffrey B. Conyers

For over 10 years you have been a source of wisdom and support for me. As I transitioned from my youth to now an established Husband, Father, and Clergyman, I can count on you to remain consistent. The past few years I have been able to accomplish several personal goals of mine but with your encouragement I enrolled into Dominion Theological Seminary and obtained my Associates in Biblical Studies. Your diligence and commitment to people have always been inspirational to me. Thank you for being one of a kind.

Toya Brown (Godmother)

You have always been a tremendous blessing to my life. Whether it was in word or deed, I appreciate your wisdom and support. I do not explain my actions or take advice from many people but your understanding of who I am and what I aim to accomplish has always been a force of momentum in my life. You have exposed me to tough love - I understand it now and embrace it.

Love you always Gma

Foreword

Better.

It has been said that sometimes the greatest victories are after some of the greater battles in life. Some of the greatest dreamers of our time, lived through some of the worst nightmares. But along came better.

In this book, we embark on a spiritual journey to wholeness, hope, and the promise of a better day. Like a coach in the heat of a game, Curtis Whiteman, through his genius, pulls us to the sideline and gives us strategy, encouragement, and empowerment to keep moving forward amidst the shuffle on the court.

Truth is, we do not always know which way to go. We get tired. We lose hope. We faint. This devotional reminds us that it is not the future that needs hope, but our heart on the journey. May you be daring enough to find the beauty of being. Better Days are not just coming…they are within.

Pastor J.J. Allen
City of Awakening, Newark, NJ

Table of Contents

Day 1

Psalms 63:1-3

1. O God, thou [art] my God; early will I seek thee: my soul thirsteth for thee, my flesh longeth for thee in a dry and thirsty land, where no water is;
2. To see thy power and thy glory, so [as] I have seen thee in the sanctuary.
3. Because thy lovingkindness [is] better than life, my lips shall praise thee.

As I converted to Christianity, I was taught the importance of prayer. Prayer is a communication between the believer and God, prayer is a daily exercise of faith. We must pray in season and out of season which means you should pray when you feel like it and when you do not.

As we look to cultivate our earthly relationships, we must look to do the same with our Creator. We can accomplish this by making prayer a consistent act in our lives. Firstly, we must realize that prayer is not a monologue - it is a dialogue. The key difference between our God and others, is that our God speaks back to us. This is a beautiful thing! While others struggle to find their place in life or for direction, our God gives us an advantage by preparing us for our daily walk with him.

Enter an intimate relationship with God by seeking him early in prayer. It is easy to become distracted and overwhelmed by life, but with time spent with your father God in prayer, you will not become overwhelmed by anxiety or fear. God is the chief therapist! Speak to God daily and leave space for him to respond to you.

Our God does not restrict or limit how we can approach him. Many times, I will pray several short prayers during my day as I am walking, as I am working, and as I am working out at the gym. The remarkable thing is that I know that even though I am not being formal, he honors the time and effort I put forward in growing our relationship. I promise you, the more you pray the more you will grow.

Today's Practice:

Before you begin your day, talk to God first. Do not check your email or social media until you ask him what his plan is for your day and ask him to direct you.

Day 2

- Proverbs 16:7

When a man's ways please the LORD, he maketh even his enemies to be at peace with him.

There is safety and blessings in living a life that is pleasing to the Lord. I believe as a people we waste too much time trying to prove our enemies wrong or even being better than our enemies, that we forget we were not created for that purpose. Our purpose is to do the Will of God that we were born to perform. Naturally, Satan will send people and traps to distract you and discourage you by making your purpose difficult to achieve. Enemies can be a person or an obstacle that fights against the Will of God that is assigned to us.

I believe that many people have become so distracted by their enemies that they have forgotten the fact that God is bigger than them. I want to share this truth with you: The devil is NOT

24

God's equal! He is in fact lower than God with no real power. He attacks and distracts with permission and under God's careful watch. So, with that said why should we entertain a powerless entity? It is foolish. Learn to refocus your attention on God and the divine purpose of your life.

All power belongs to God and with God on your side victory is only a matter of time for you. I encourage you to turn your face from your enemies and focus your vision on God. Our scripture of the day teaches us when we make God happy, he makes those that hate us swallow their pride and know that God's blessings are with us.

Today's Practice:

Find a way to please God today. Whether it be through a kind act to another person, or speaking to him (God)

Day 3

- Proverbs 29:11

A fool uttereth all his mind: but a wise [man] keepeth it in till afterwards.

I recall a saying as I was growing up "Never let your left hand know what your right hand is doing". I tend to have a literal mind so I could not comprehend what this saying meant, but as I grew older and had more interactions with people, I quickly learned the meaning.

Many times, we block our progress and blessings by speaking either too much, or prematurely. It is best to let the Lord finish working on your behalf before you reveal the blessing you received. Please do not be ignorant to the fact that everyone you share your good news with is not rooting for you.

Sharing good news with the wrong people can delay a blessing. The negative words spoken over your life by an enemy in disguise prolongs the arrival of what God promised you. In the Book of Daniel, Chapter 10, the angel said he heard the prayer the first day and was released to respond but he came across opposition. Catch this point if you are sharing your blessings and secrets with people that are not assisting you in prayer - their negative words could serve as an opposition to it as well. I challenge you to be a Wise man/woman by holding it to yourself until God completes the work.

Today's Practice:

Practice restraint. Ask God who you should, and when you should, share your thoughts and feelings, and whom you should share it with. Be wise in this delicate decision you are about to make. Your blessings and plans being revealed to the wrong person can hinder its progress.

Day 4

- Proverbs 21:23

Whoso keepeth his mouth and his tongue keepeth his soul from troubles.

Most times it is best to keep your mouth shut. In recent years we allowed access to podcasts, blogs, and social media to strip us of the discernment to know when to speak up and when to remain silent on an issue. Every situation does not require your insight on it. It is better to remain ignorant to some events than to be knowledgeable and speak on something that you are not completely informed of.

It takes a high level of maturity to understand what issues are not up for discussion. The fact that you have an opinion does not qualify you to express them. During my years in the workforce, I have witnessed many people called into a conference at their place of employment, not because they were directly involved, but because they decided to express themselves on the topic at hand to the wrong people and at the wrong time. Please understand that my plea to everyone is to learn that there is peace in silence. Do not ever put your peace in jeopardy because of a lack of self-discipline.

We possess the ability to create change in our daily lives with the words we speak. Be careful not to destroy what you are trying to build, with your words.

Today's Practice:

Examine your responses to people and situations before you speak, by asking yourself "will my next statement create or destroy?"

Day 5

[He that is] slow to anger [is] better than the mighty; and he that ruleth his spirit than he that taketh a city.

When a person reacts in anger, they reveal the lack of discipline present in their lives. Various times, in anger, thoughts and feelings are expressed in a cruel and harsh way. A man or woman of peace positions themselves to not react in anger, but rather with discipline and self-control. When you rule your own spirit, control and power is shifted into your hands.

The reason I used the word "react" is that people who react are usually impulsive, while people that respond are usually calculated and prepared. A person who reacts, tends to put many aspects of their lives in danger because of their actions. I asked you passionately to respond to conflict instead of reacting.

Your next response to a difficult situation can put you in a tough spot if you choose anger. Make sure you have exhausted all your options before you escalate to a place of anger.

Today's Practice:

During your day, challenge yourself to respond instead of reacting. Afterward reflect on how the situation might have ended differently if you had reacted.

Day 6

- Ecclesiastes 10:19

A feast is made for laughter, and wine maketh merry: but money answereth all [things].

As a child I was wrongly taught "Money is the root of all evil" but as I matured in the Lord, I discovered that the scripture (1st Timothy 6:10), was being misquoted. I always questioned, how can something that is so important be evil? Money in many cultures, is a topic people avoid discussing -possibly out of ignorance of how to increase their income, or paranoia that details will be revealed regarding their personal finances. Although I encourage everyone to be wise in whom they reveal details to, I also encourage them not to be scared to discuss finances.

Lack of financial wisdom is dangerous to your future. I urge every reader of this devotional to begin to aggressively save for your future. Although we trust God with our future, we must be prepared for any financial hardship that might occur down the road. A wise man once told me to save and invest for my future. He challenged me to be wise about where I place my money. I have made it common practice to watch my spending patterns and stay within my created budget.

Today's Practice:

Can you survive within 80% of your income?

It is customary practice to tithe in the Christian faith. As a savings technique, tithe to your savings accounts and do not spend it! The remaining 80% will be for you to maintain your monthly expenses. I believe if you cannot survive off the remaining 80% you should consider lowering your expenses.

Day 7

- Psalms 37:1-3

1. Fret not thyself because of evildoers, Neither be thou envious against the workers of iniquity.

2. For they shall soon be cut down like the grass, And wither as the green herb.

3. Trust in the LORD, and do good; So shalt thou dwell in the land, and verily thou shalt be fed.

I believe at some point every believer has looked at the life of a "worker of iniquity" and compared themselves to that life. It is important to know that although it might appear that they are prospering, that image is only a façade. Our faith goes deeper than what our eyes can see and what our minds can comprehend. Although it might appear that all is well, in due time they will fall.

I beg you to do as the scripture says by trusting in the Lord and doing good. There must be an

49

establishment of trust in your relationship with the Lord. Your reaping of good days is only a matter of time. Endure this season of waiting and you will benefit greatly when the Lord releases his blessings to you. The second command of this scripture is to "do good". When your reaping season comes, you can be sure that good things will come into your life. Do good unto people when you can – even when you do not feel like it.

Today's Practice:

You might see some prosperous evildoers, but I challenge you to see how much more the Lord has caused you to prosper. You will appreciate what God has done for you when you stop focusing on what he is doing for others. As you embark on your day write down one way the Lord has blessed you.

Day 8

- Proverbs 15:29

*The LORD is far from the wicked: But he heareth
the prayer of the righteous.*

There will be times in your relationship with God
when you might think that he is not hearing you.
The fact is however, that if you are in right
standing with the Lord, he will always be near to
you. A person might wonder, "how do I keep the
Lord near me?". Sin and wickedness create a
barrier between us and God. As loving and
forgiving as God is, he will not leave us, but he
will step back from us until we repent and get
back on track. We are given the choice to obey
and be safe in the will of God or rebel and remain
unprotected.

I believe that if you want the Lord to remain near,
you must be righteous. Righteous is defined as

virtuous, morally right, or justifiable. Remaining righteous as the verse states, puts your prayers in a position to be heard and answered. Being righteous is not about pointing out the errors of others, rather it is about being able to identify what is wrong or immoral and doing what is right. Stand on the side of what is right, and the Lord will stand alongside you throughout your life. It was never promised that life would be easy, but with God present, you will make it through every season of life - both pleasant and challenging.

Today's Practice:

Position yourself for a lifestyle of righteousness by being virtuous, morally right, or justifiable. Today, if the opportunity presents itself, be righteous by doing the right thing even if pressured to do what is easy and wrong

Day 9

- *Deuteronomy 24:16*

The fathers shall not be put to death for the children, neither shall the children be put to death for the fathers: every man shall be put to death for his own sin.

In many circles of Christianity, the topic of "generational curses" is mentioned and discussed in detail. For the sake of those that have never heard of this term, I will explain it to the best of my ability. A generational curse can be a situation or circumstance that seems to attack a family from generation to generation. Perhaps the women of a family pass away from breast cancer, or several members of a family have passed away due to violence. Those are a few examples of generational curses. Make no mistake about it, generational curses are from the devil

Generational curses do not have to be a part of

your life or your family's. You do not have to sit and suffer while the devil attacks you and your family. Many might teach that the curse on a family started with the sin or error of an individual which resulted in the attacks the family experiences. I want you to take comfort in this fact - you are not paying for your father's sins. It is unfair and unrealistic to have to carry and repent for the sins of former generations. Your sins are heavy enough. It is not God's will for you to carry someone else's as well. If that was God's will, the death, burial, and resurrection of Jesus Christ was for nothing. I believe what the bible says, and that is that he (Jesus) carried my sins on the cross and died for/with them.

Please understand my premise I am not saying generational curses do not exist, rather I am saying you do not have to live under the deception that you are defenseless. We have a weapon against all curses - fasting and prayer. I challenge you to use your weapons of fasting and prayer.

Today's Practice:

Look over your family history and if you notice a generational curse pray against it continuing. It is time as a believer of Christ, that we go on the offensive and attack rather than defend ourselves. Pray with passion over your family. Pray that no more members of your family (immediate and extended) will fall to the spirit that is attacking. Pray with your family; there is power in numbers.

Day 10

He that [hath] no rule over his own spirit [is like] a city [that is] broken down, [and] without walls.

Control of your attitude and temper in life is key to your development as a person. Lack of self-control exposes a person as an individual with poor character and principles. It is important to maintain your composure under pressure, and not put your reputation in jeopardy. A reputation as "hotheaded" is not ideal for any individual.

As an individual who has learned how to "rule over his own spirit" I have seen firsthand the benefit of self-control. In moments of anger, there is little thought of the consequences of our actions, both short-term and long-term. In those moments of reckless response, just as the city mentioned in the scriptures, you are left defenseless; you are left defenseless to what will be said about you and the opportunities you will lose from your actions.

I want to take this moment and speak to your humanity; you will have moments of anger in life, but it is your choice of how you respond. Do not let a moment of anger or immaturity cause you to forfeit a blessing that God has in store for you. God has great things in mind for your future, but he will not manifest it if he cannot trust you to control your urge to react irresponsibly.

Today's Practice:

Look for an opportunity to respond to a difficult situation in a different way. There will be times you will be challenged to respond with anger and sarcasm, instead respond with patience and love. Remember, your response can either deliver your blessing or postpone it.

Day 11

- James 1:17

Every good gift and every perfect gift is from above, and cometh down from the Father of lights, with whom is no variableness, neither shadow of turning.

God has invested a gift into all of us. The gift God has given to you, was designed to change lives and direct all praise back to him. In today's culture, so many people envy the gifts of others but neglect the development of the gift God gave them. Upon discovery of your gift, it is up to you to use your gift for his purpose. I encourage you to use your God-given gift today to help or inspire someone else.

Our gifts present the ability to open doors of opportunity and wealth if we take proper care of, and further develop them. God did his part by investing the gifts into each of us, but we must do

69

our part by nurturing and studying those gifts.

The more you comprehend and honor what God gave you, the better you will be able use that gift.

Today's Practice:

My plea to you today is to acknowledge your gift and further develop it to perfection. Your gift can change the world.

Day 12

- 1 Corinthians 15:57

But thanks be to God, which giveth us the victory through our Lord Jesus Christ.

As believers of Christ, we are guaranteed victory over every roadblock, distraction, and circumstance. Before we decided to follow Christ, we had to fight alone, and victory was not guaranteed. As the scripture stated, "But thanks be to God,", we no longer fight alone but now we have the backing of our Lord and Savior Jesus Christ working with and for us daily. The pressure of winning is one many fall to, but as believers we no longer need to handle that pressure alone.

When times get hard and you feel overwhelmed, remember that the Lord Jesus Christ is with you, and you will win. You can do more with Jesus than you ever could alone. I encourage you to never forget that victory comes through our connection to Jesus. God has a plan for each of our lives and through fellowship, with Jesus Christ, we will all fulfill the purpose we were created for.

Today's Practice:

Examine your recent challenges and recall how Jesus brought victory to you, afterward thank him for doing it.

Day 13

- 2 Corinthians 4:16

For which cause we faint not; but though our outward man perish, yet the inward man is renewed day by day.

God is eternal; he is timeless. God is a spirit and so are we. We are spirits placed in a body. This body can go through changes, it can deteriorate and diminish, but the spirit remains strong. After we pass away our spirits live on. Do not be confused! We (me and you) are spiritual beings! It is imperative to strengthen your spirit as well as your body. Your survival is dependent upon your desire to strengthen your spirit.

Many have worked on their bodies and wardrobe but forgot to perform maintenance on their spirit. Your spiritual health is vital to your survival in life. I plead with you to renew your inward man. You

might wonder "how do I renew my inward man?".
It is simple - you renew your inward man through
a relationship with God. If you make prayer,
fasting, and biblical study a part of your life
consistently, your inward man will be renewed. A
renewed spirit is a strong spirit. Renew your spirit
to endure the ups and downs life will present to
you.

Today's practice:

We exist in this world in body, but our authority is in heavenly places. Today I challenge you to exercise your spiritual authority by speaking to a dilemma or situation that appears to not be in your favor. Pray on it and command it to change.

Day 14

- *Colossians 3:13*

Forbearing one another, and forgiving one another, if any man have a quarrel against any: even as Christ forgave you, so also do ye.

I have noticed many things in my journey as a Christian, one of them is that people will often want to be forgiven for their mistakes but lack the compassion to forgive others. Much like love, forgiveness must be reciprocated from one party to the next. Remember, we reap the same thing that we sow to others. There will come a time where you will desire to be forgiven but you will reap that act at the same speed you have sown it. The great thing about forgiveness is you can forgive someone for an act or deed whether they know it or not.

The act of forgiveness is to your benefit. As believers of Christ, we must live free of hatred and offense - your progression in life depends on how fast you are willing to let go of the offenses that have been holding you back. Do not let the other party move on and be happy while you stay stuck in the past; free yourself and move on too. Stop letting people live rent-free in your spirit, that is where God should reside! When you hold onto offense and grudges you are carrying that person around in your heart. Do not let a bad experience bring bitterness into your life. My prayer for you is that you will release this matter to God.

Today's Practice:

Forgive the offenses that you keep replaying in your heart and mind. You have thought about it too many times and deserve the liberty of living an offense-free life.

Day 15

- Mark 11:24

Therefore I say unto you, What things soever ye desire, when ye pray, believe that ye receive them, and ye shall have them.

The scripture reveals two simple steps to getting what your heart desires. The first is we must pray. It does us no good to tell our dreams and goals to anyone but God, because he is able to open the doors for us. The second step mentioned in the scripture is to believe. If you ask for something from God and you do not believe, you may have wasted your time. You must believe that what you asked for in prayer can, and will, happen for you at its appointed time.

I cannot emphasize the importance of prayer in the life of a Christian believer. Your prayer life is essential to your existence. When the world comes against you there is strength found in prayer. Through prayer, there is also direction and identity found. People wander through life with many questions concerning their purpose and future. My thought is "why not ask your creator for answers?" If I bought an item and I was unsure of its purpose and how to use it, I would contact the manufacturer. I believe in the same logic applies to our lives. When you have questions and concerns about your life you should go directly to God and ask questions. Prayer is a small act that can create a large impact.

As a believer of Christ, faith is a requirement. Our Bible tells us that "without faith, it is impossible to please God". If you desire to obtain what you prayed for you must first believe. Prayer is a simple dialogue between yourself, and God. Do not be afraid to talk to God and make a request, he has your best interest at heart. God does not require your faith to be at one hundred percent to work a miracle for you, but he does need a portion of it.

Today's Practice:

Consider something that you always wanted to do or accomplish, then pray for and about it. You are one prayer away from success; keep praying.

Day 16

- Galatians 6:10

As we have therefore opportunity, let us do good unto all [men], especially unto them who are of the household of faith.

As believers of Christ, we are challenged daily to live by a standard of integrity, kindness, and service to others. Many people outside of the faith will unfairly judge us by those same principles without merit. One of my strongest convictions is to "do good", because people will remember how you treat them and how you made them feel. It cost nothing to be kind - whether by way of an encouraging word or act of support. Extend kind acts to all men during our lifetime.

As we all progress and ascend in life we have an opportunity, and a duty to pay it forward. In other words, as somebody has helped you it is now your duty to help others. I wholeheartedly believe in the principle of sowing and reaping; it is how we cycle blessings from one another. It is unfortunate that many people do not look for the opportunity to be a blessing to another person. As believers, we miss the opportunity to be a blessing almost daily. Someone is depending on our kindness to get them to the next level. Do not miss that opportunity to be a blessing.

Today's practice:

Look for an opportunity to perform a good act for someone. Being used by God to bless a life is an honor. Be open to blessing both strangers and friends.

- *Proverbs 11:14*

Where no counsel is, the people fall: but in the multitude of counsellors there is safety.

I am a fan of wisdom. Whenever there is wisdom being shared, I posture myself to be taught. I do as scripture advises by being slow to speak and fast to listen. Your posture, while wisdom is being shared, will determine the trajectory of your future. Wisdom costs the adviser time, money, stress, and heartache, but it costs nothing for the recipient of that wisdom to remain humble enough to accept the offered wisdom.

Simply put when you avoid or run from wisdom, failure is guaranteed. It is to your benefit to accept the wisdom that is offered to you. The only thing wisdom will cost you is time - I believe that is a fair trade-off. I am certain we all, at some point, may have made the mistake of not seeking the counsel of the wise. Do not repeat the error of thinking you know best! God will always provide you with insight and information, but we must accept it when God brings it to us.

Today's Practice:

You will have several conversations today, whether at home, work, or school. Be open to wisdom in your casual conversations. This can come from the people you least expect but have an ear for that wisdom in any situation.

Day 18

- Hebrews 12:15

Looking diligently lest any man fail of the grace of God; lest any root of bitterness springing up trouble [you], and thereby many be defiled;

Life can serve us many things, most of them unexpected. While we suffer through many ups and downs, we are prone to become bitter because of those moments. Bitterness comes from unresolved issues.

You have the right to process your trauma in whatever fashion you want however you cannot allow your trauma to make you bitter. Bitterness is a state of being that many, shockingly, do not realize they are currently in. As a healthy individual, you must evaluate your mental health as well as your current state of being. As a believer, you need to be free from bitterness so you can accept the blessings God has planned for you.

Often bitter people tend to project their bitterness onto people unaware and unfairly. The one thing I find interesting about bitterness is the bitter party shares it with others. The scripture says bitterness defiles many and if you're not paying attention, it will do great harm to others. Bitterness will often be the root in a person who attacks and offends others. Sometimes, bitterness even recruits other bitter people into its company. Be careful that whatever disappointments and trauma you have experienced do not result in seeds of bitterness in your life. It is God's desire that we move from bitter to better and be free!

Today's Practice:

Release your bitterness to God. Ask God in prayer to reveal your areas of bitterness You are one prayer closer to complete healing of past hurt. Do not hide from it or avoid it, rather address it and heal.

Day 19

- Mark 12:31

And the second is like, namely this, Thou shalt love thy neighbour as thyself. There is none other commandment greater than these.

Love is an emotion and action that is often used very loosely. To give love, a person must first understand what love is, and how to properly show it. I believe that to effectively give love you must know how to receive it first. From birth, every person is taught directly and indirectly about love by way of the relationships they form or the relationships they observe. We become the product of the foundation we are raised under.

Contrary to some theories, love can be taught. Many attach to unhealthy relationships because they witnessed poor examples of love. When poor examples are the standard of our lives, we begin to accept abnormal conditions as normal. I will state this confidently "love does not hurt intentionally". Abuse should never become normal or acceptable, God desires more for you, and you should too.

We all must define what love is, my terms and definition of love might differ from the next person. The key is learning to show love to one another within the next person's guidelines. If a person has difficulty accepting love for any reason it will become very challenging to do as the scripture says in "loving thy neighbor as thyself". Love starts from within; you cannot share what is not inside of you.

Love yourself. Respect yourself. Appreciate yourself. Invest in yourself. If you can do these things without shortchanging yourself, you can certainly love your neighbor.

Today's Practice:

Show Love: You may encounter many new faces today. Make a strong effort to show love to each of them. You can show love by an act of kindness or simply by being the friend that you wish you had, to them.

Day 20

And the key of the house of David will I lay upon his shoulder; so he shall open, and none shall shut; and he shall shut, and none shall open.

No person, no devil, or no distraction can get in the way of God's plan for your life. God is in total control of which doors open and close in your life. You must find peace in the fact that God is in control and not yourself. Our God knows what is best for us in our immediate and long-term future.

Doors are entryways to rooms. Many of us are trying to unlock doors that God did not purpose for you to open. Do not fight against God's plan for your life. If you are destined to enter the room God will provide access to you. Not being given access is not necessarily a bad thing. For many, being locked out of a room is protection from embarrassment, trauma, and wasted resources.

114

You should celebrate a closed door as much as you celebrate an open door. As I have aged, I have learned to not force open a door that seems closed. I have also learned to be willing to accept whatever happens. You do not want to force God's hand to give you something that was not in his plan. Become comfortable waiting on God to reveal his decision. What God has in store for you is better than what you could ever plan. Trust that it will be perfect.

Today's Practice:

Give up. Surrender your plan for God's plan. His will is perfect and meant to bring you to a prosperous place. Ask God to reveal to you what doors are meant to be opened and what doors are meant to be closed. Asking this will save you from heartache and wasted time. Pursue the door that truly belongs to you.

Day 21

- Matthew 6:34

Take therefore no thought for the morrow: for the morrow shall take thought for the things of itself. Sufficient unto the day [is] the evil thereof.

It is completely normal to worry about the unknown. Worry comes into play when we realize we lack control, or we do not know the outcome of a situation. Worry does not resolve the matter at hand, in fact, it makes it worse. As a believer, we have a source that will relieve the stress and worry from our minds. God did not intend for you to worry about tomorrow, he intends for you to plan for tomorrow.

As a believer, I leave my worry and concerns in prayer. After I express my thoughts and feelings to God, I make a conscious effort to leave those issues in God's hands. Tomorrow is always on the way; it is always coming. If tomorrow is on your schedule, you have time to accomplish what you envisioned for yourself.

When you have God, you have time. Leave tomorrow and the worries of it with him because the issues and concerns of tomorrow can only be handled by him.

Today's Practice:

Tomorrow is a big day for you, consider the things that cause you anxiety and stress. Your assignment is before you worry about tomorrow, pray about tomorrow and hand your worries over to God.

Day 22

- *Joshua 1:9*

Have not I commanded thee? Be strong and of a good courage; be not afraid, neither be thou dismayed: for the Lord thy God is with thee whithersoever thou goest.

Life at times can be oppressing, depressing, and even traumatic but with God, we are set up for victory. The thought of suffering through life's challenges is not your reality; God is guiding and leading you every step of the way. I look at life through the lens of optimism instead of focusing on problems, setbacks, and situations. I choose to focus on the solution which is found in my relationship with God. I have confidence in God's ability to work things out for me.

There's nothing you and God cannot do together; the Lord is with you. I find peace in knowing that

124

all I need to do is face whatever life throws at me and God will support me with his grace. Whatever challenges and situations you may encounter, all you must do is face it directly. Take comfort in the fact that God is right by your side from the very beginning. Continue to be strong and courageous, as children of God we do not have to fight alone.

Today's Practice:

Face the challenges of your day without fear. When we face our challenges without faith, we open the door to fear walking in. Be confident in the fact that God is with you during every challenge of life.

Day 23

- Philippians 4:9

Those things, which ye have both learned, and received, and heard, and seen in me, do: and the God of peace shall be with you.

Life is all about lessons! It has a way of teaching us what we need to learn in both subtle and sometimes drastic ways. Much like school, if we do not catch the lesson that life is trying to teach us, we will have to endure that lesson until we master the concept. Do not try to avoid the lessons, they are ordained for your life.

One thing I consider to be fun is the journey to discovering the lesson. The process of learning what God is trying to develop in each of us is as important as the lesson. Becoming who God created you to be is not an overnight process, it takes a lifetime to learn your purpose and then to become the best version of yourself possible. Being anything less than what God has purposed for you is unsatisfactory.

Today's Practice:

Embrace the lessons you have learned while in the faith. Our faith has many lessons to share with us; it is not good enough to simply know the lessons and rules, we must live by them. Today while you are experiencing life, exercise a lesson you are learning.

- Proverbs 17:17

A friend loveth at all times, And a brother is born for adversity.

I believe friendship is a gift from God. At any given moment a person should be able to gain strength, wisdom, and empowerment from their circle of friends. True friendships endure the many ups and downs of life. In life, you need a strong support system to carry you to where God destined you to be.

Friends are the family you choose to bring into your life. You cannot pick your siblings, but you can pick who you call "bro" or "sis"...be wise in that decision. Do not recklessly give those titles out because it requires a lifetime commitment. It is easy to be a friend during good times but when adversity arises brotherhood is needed.

Commit to your relationships beyond your disagreements and feelings. As a brother, I may not agree with decisions that are being made with my brothers and sister, but my love for them does not change. When your family becomes weary you must be strong on their behalf. Support each other as we should.

Today's Practice:

Be a brother or sister to somebody. We all know of somebody that is facing tough times, support them by being present. Your text message, phone call, or visit can be more encouraging than you think.

Day 25

- Proverbs 4:23

Keep thy heart with all diligence; For out of it are the issues of life.

One of my daily practices is to protect my heart and mind from those that will hurt me, both intentionally and accidentally. Over the course of my life, I have noticed that whatever I allowed to penetrate my heart and mind, I then became. Simply said, you will become what you allow into your spirit. I believe that if you allow love to flow freely in your life, you will be able to freely reciprocate.

You must take responsibility for what you allow to penetrate your heart; you do not have to settle for envy, hatred, and loneliness. As children of God, we are entitled to the best and that includes our emotional health. I want to encourage every reader to not settle for negativity when positivity is promised to you.

The heart has a way of expressing itself and it tends to do it without permission of the mind. Think about some of the conversations you have had. I am certain either you or the other party have "slipped up" and said something that revealed how they felt. Remember this: The heart is selfish and whether it is hurting or in a healthy state, it will speak its truth. Your job is to make sure the condition of your heart remains pure.

Today's Practice:

Protect your heart with passion. Make every effort to reject negative words that might be spoken over your life. Remember whatever you allow into your spirit is what you will become.

Day 26

- Isaiah 64:8

But now, O LORD, thou art our father; we are the clay, and thou our potter; and we all are the work of thy hand.

A potter's job is to mold clay into whatever object they envisioned as they began their work. As children of God, we must be as clay by not fighting against our molding process. Truthfully, being molded can be a painful process but fighting against the molding process can be even more strenuous.

I would challenge every reader of this book to embrace your molding process. Let God shape you and even burn out every impurity that lies dormant in you. Our fathers' goal in molding us is that our image would reflect him. Your process might be longer than others but do not forget the purpose of getting on God's wheel as clay.

144

One lesson I must deliver in this book is to stay in the hands of God. There is nowhere in the world safer than God's hands. Being in God's hands is equivalent to being in God's will for your life. When you are living and functioning in his will, you are in a safe and prosperous state. Everything you need will be provided for you when you are in right standing with God.

Today's Practice:

Remain moldable by God. God has a way of shaping us and modeling us for his purpose. When you fight against that process you forfeit the blessings attached to your purpose.

Day 27

- 1 John 4:7

Beloved, let us love one another: for love is of God; and every one that loveth is born of God, and knoweth God.

Love is a noun, it's an action word! It must be put on display and not just in words. Anybody can say the words "I love you" to you, but you know the love is real when there is action placed behind those words. Love can be challenging but it has the strength to endure many storms when it is genuine.

When love is in your heart it will lead you to do right by and for people. We must show love to one another even when it hurts. All healthy families show love daily to each other. As believers we inherit additional brothers and sisters in the faith, therefore we must love each other as family.

149

It is not possible to love God and not love his people. We are commanded to love each other because God is love. Showing love is a sign that you are a follower of God. Without showing those signs, it becomes difficult to identify you as a believer. Signs are used to identify what is to come down the road, so make sure you are showing signs of love when people encounter you. Failure to show love results in not being identified as a believer of Christ.

Today's Practice:

Learn to love people as God loves us. Be tolerant, forgiving, and most of all be real with your love.

Day 28

- Philippians 4:11

Not that I speak in respect of want: for I have learned, in whatsoever state I am, [therewith] to be content.

It is natural to desire the best things that life has to offer; most people feel that they deserve those things. There is nothing wrong with wanting the best out of life that is what I call a "justified desire". In all my years of living, I have never met any person who desired to struggle and live below their means. I believe that God places your desires in your heart as a preview for what is to come in your life.

My concern with desires is the reaction to waiting for them to come into existence. Your attitude and perception can either expedite or delay your dreams from becoming a reality. The key to the waiting process is being content. Whatever phase of life you are in learn to be content. All of us must learn to make the most of our present. While you are waiting on the promises of God, you should be planning and preparing for what he has shown you that is coming.

We must not allow our content heart to kill our desire, there is a balance. You should continue to dream and plan for your future. God has a plan for each of us and through the ups and downs of life, we will achieve them all.

Today's Practice:

Appreciate your current situation. Compare where you are now to where you were several years ago. There is a chance that you have grown and advanced over the years. You are on the journey to greatness so embrace the process and appreciate your growth.

- Matthew 5:16

Let your light so shine before men, that they may see your good works, and glorify your Father which is in heaven.

People will remember a person by their deeds and how they make others feel. As believers, we represent our father in heaven with every word we speak and every action we make. Our behavior reflects God's character. In our lives, some people cannot separate man's character flaws from what they believe about God. This action is unfair but very common so it imperative all believers have good character.

Every believer should be a light in the darkness; we bring the love and character of God everywhere we go. Your daily interactions with people will reveal God's heart, so our deeds must speak well of our savior. Every one of our actions should bring glory to God, and the people we encounter should see God's glory reflected in your life.

Today's Practice:

Do not dim your light...do something good for someone. Remember our deeds reflect God's love through us. The things we do for others shows the love that God has for them also.

Day 30

- Proverbs 21:21

*He that followeth after righteousness and mercy
Findeth life, righteousness, and honour.*

In other translations of this scripture, the reader is
encouraged to follow righteousness and love. To
be righteous is to be morally correct. As
believers, we must do what is right in the eyes of
God. Many times, if we analyze life through our
eyes of humanity what is seen will not mirror what
God sees. To be righteous, we must know God
and his attributes. Becoming familiar with God is
not a difficult task. It can be accomplished with
prayer, reading Gods' Word (Bible), and fasting. If
you can commit to a lifestyle of learning God, you
can achieve righteousness.

I believe that love and mercy go hand in hand -
they are partners. In any relationship whether it is

164

romantic, platonic, or professional, we all must extend grace to the other party in moments of turmoil and offense.

Present in this scripture is the principle of sowing and reaping. When we give (sow) we should look to receive (reap) in many ways from God. It is our choice to sow wisely or recklessly. When you decide to live morally correct and show love you should expect a quality life and honor in return.

Today's Practice:

Commit to a lifestyle of morality and love. Make every effort today to consistently show love and be righteous. The next season of your life depends on the decision to include both in your daily life. Righteousness and love are lifestyle choices...choose well.

Day 31

- Psalm 73:26 KJV

My flesh and my heart faileth: But God is the strength of my heart, and my portion for ever.

Personally, I think as believers we depend on our intelligence and feelings to navigate our lives. Unfortunately, we forget to consult with God about the events in our lives as we should. The best thing anybody can do is to consult God for direction first. Way too often we depend on God's leading **after** we realize the answer is not within us.

Our goal should be to become full of God and allow him to enter your heart. It is impossible to make a mistake when God is leading you every step of the way. There will be many times God will try to speak to you, and he usually begins in your heart. When you say things like "something told me" or "I had a feeling" you should recognize that is God speaking to your heart.

God starts speaking to the heart to compel you. Whatever issue or concern you are considering you should know you are carrying it around in your heart. God cares about the matters of your heart, please do not forget that. Your life and concerns matter to God.

Todays Practice:

Your assignment today is simply to depend on the strength of God. As people we tend to lean on our own understanding and strength to complete our task. Life can be stressful and sometimes even inconvenient but when you depend on God's wisdom and strength, all things are made easy.

Day 32
BONUS DAY

- *Ephesians 3:20*

Now unto him that is able to do exceeding abundantly above all that we ask or think, according to the power that worketh in us,

One lesson I have been blessed to learn throughout my course in Christianity is God has an incredible imagination. We as his children tend to limit God to our level. God is much larger than the box we are limited to, but we miss out on many blessings because our views and faith are limited.

God created the Heavens, earth, and everything on the earth within seven days. He did all of this with his imagination; there was no example to follow. In the beginning, God was what we call today, a "Creative". When you are a creative person, you think on a different level because your mind is operating at a higher capacity than others.

Although we are made in the image of God our minds do not operate on his level. God knows the roadmap of each of our lives. He is aware of every U-turn and detour you will have to make in your journey. It is best that as we are on our journey, we consult God for precise directions because he knows the road you are on.

My key life acknowledgment is that God is bigger than I am. I humbly submit to his plan, and I refuse to fight against his purpose for my life. I trust that his plan is better than what I can imagine.

Today's Practice:

Do not limit God's blessings to your box. Ask God to perform a miracle for you today and do not try to figure out how it will happen. My challenge to you today, is to think bigger and ask for bigger.

About the Author

Prophet Curtis Dennis Whiteman was born and raised in the Bedford-Stuyvesant section of Brooklyn, NY. Curtis is the second of three children from the Union of Irvin Whiteman, Sr, and Martina Whiteman. He was the most boring kid you would have ever met, ordinary in every sense of the word. Then something special happened to him, he met the Lord at the age of thirteen. Through middle school he was an underachiever until he encountered and learned about Jesus Christ.

In 1998, after a moving message on self-esteem, Curtis gave his life to the Lord, and it was in that moment his spiritual mother Apostle Patricia Wiley, ministered to him about the call on his life. Curtis accepted Christ and served at Resurrection Temple of Our Lord in Brooklyn, NY under the leadership of Bishop Wesley Wiley from 1998 to 2011, where he gained a deeper understanding of Jesus Christ and service unto the Lord. He served in many roles but mainly as Adjutant, Sound

Technician and Public Relations/Media President.

In December of 2015, the Lord sent Curtis back home to Apostle Wiley, and the Oil of Joy Ministries II family. Under the tutelage of Apostle Wiley, he has developed his prophetic gift and is steadily going to deeper depths and higher heights in his calling. Curtis loves to share the Word of God through teaching and counsel. In September of 2017, Curtis became a licensed Associate Minister at Oil of Joy Ministries II; at this time he also founded the Servant Institute - which is a Leadership training conference for Servants of the Local household of Faith.

In 2020 Prophet Whiteman released his first book entitled *Foundations of the Prophetic* which has been used as a tool for instruction and spiritual growth for all prophetic believers. Shortly after the release of *Foundations of the Prophetic*, the Lord ministered to Prophet Whiteman regarding building and maintaining healthy relationships in the faith. During this time, he wrote his now released second book *Elijah's Heir*.

Prophet Curtis Whiteman is a husband of one to Pastor Andrea Shaw-Whiteman, and the proud father of two young children - Samuel Chauncey and Adrianna Janae. In June of 2022 Prophet Curtis Whiteman will receive his bachelor's degree in Biblical Studies. He is on his way to becoming Dr. Curtis Whiteman. His favorite scripture is Isaiah 59:1 "Behold, the LORD'S hand is not shortened, that it cannot save; neither his ear heavy, that it cannot hear."